W9-BNC-556

Sports Illustrated
TENNIS

The Sports Illustrated Library

Sports Illustrated
TENNIS

By BILL TALBERT
and the Editors of
Sports Illustrated

Illustrations by
Ed Vebell

J. B. LIPPINCOTT COMPANY
Philadelphia and New York

U.S. Library of Congress Cataloging in Publication Data

Talbert, William F
    Sports illustrated tennis.

    (Sports illustrated library)
    First ed. by the editors of Sports illustrated issued in
1961 under title: Sports illustrated book of tennis.
    1. Tennis. I. Vebell, Ed, illus. II. Sports illustrated
(Chicago) Sports illustrated book of tennis. III. Title.
GV995.T318   1972   796.34'22   72-37609
ISBN-0-397-00863-5
ISBN-0-397-00862-7 (pbk)

The following articles by Bill Talbert are reprinted from *Sports Illustrated* in slightly revised form: "How to Serve and Win" (July 5, 1965); "A Better Way to Net Play" (July 13, 1964); "The Strategies of Singles" (June 4, 1962); and "A One-Two Punch for the Prettiest" (April 15, 1963).

Photographs from *Sports Illustrated,* © Time Inc.

Cover: Al Freni

Page 77: Buck Peters

Page 85: Jerry Cooke

Contents

Sports Illustrated
TENNIS

1
Singles

PLAYERS READY? PLAY!

TENNIS is a game anyone can play. Swinging a tennis racket properly comes just as easily and naturally as throwing a ball or swatting a fly or performing any of the other untutored everyday movements that are virtually automatic. So the fun you get out of the game depends directly on how much effort you are willing to devote to memorizing and perfecting the simple tenets of the four basic shots— the serve, the forehand, the backhand and the volley.

In this opening section I have set down and interpreted, step by step, the way Donald Budge, one of the truly great champions of all time, plays these shots. There are, of course, limitless variations, and these you will learn with practice and competition—just as in dancing you embellish the simple fox trot into the rumba, the tango or the samba. But first, learn the fundamentals as they are demonstrated by one of the two men who scored the grand slam of tennis by winning the Australian, French, Wimbledon and U.S. championships in the same year (1938).

I would not want to imply that anyone can become a champion—even of the local club—just by imitating Budge. Like any competitive game, tennis involves far more than technique—for instance, temperament, concentration and the will to win. Yet these are of little significance if you don't have the proper strokes. The strokes are the weapons of tennis. Without them you are not even equipped for the battle.

The payoff on a good tennis stroke, as with a good boxing punch, depends on how much of the body's power can be compressed and unleashed—like a tightly wound spring—and thrown behind the shot. This means coordination—of feet, knees, hips, hands and shoulders. So it is worth repeating that you will achieve this coordination—once you have mastered the technique of the stroke—only through *practice*. Fine, you may say, but suppose there is no one around to practice with. The answer to that is: Use a backboard as much as possible; it is the practice fairway of tennis and many of the finest players have polished their shots against it.

Now begin the lessons, preferably learning the fundamentals one stroke at a time. If you do, you will be surprised how much more fun you will have on the court, no matter what kind of company you play in.

THE GRIP

Most of today's leading players use the eastern grip on all forehand shots, making an eighth of a turn of hand and fingers to the left to hit the backhand and serve. The advantage of this grip is that it is the most comfortable, easiest to switch from forehand to backhand and most convenient for both high and low strokes. There are, however, some acceptable variations, such as the western grip favored by the great champion Bill Johnston and the continental grip that Fred Perry used so effectively. Yet each of these

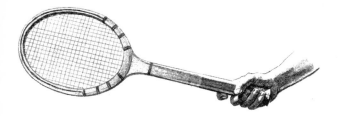

Figure 1. The Forehand Grip.

Shaking hands with the racket is a good way to assume this grip, making sure the handle extends behind the heel of the hand. Important: the grip is the one and only contact between you and the ball, so make it firm.

Figure 2. The Backhand Grip.

Hand on top of the racket with the V between the thumb and the forefinger pointing to the left shoulder at impact is the proper position for this grip—also used for the serve. For ground strokes, extend the thumb back of the handle for support.

presents its problems: The western can be extremely awkward for low shots, and the continental deprives you of power. Whichever grip you may use, the basic mechanics of the shots described on the following pages remain the same. And so, only a couple of fundamental precepts are mandatory: (1) once the shot has been decided upon, never change the grip, and (2) always relax the grip between shots to avoid tiring your hand and arm.

HOW TO SERVE AND WIN

There is no question that the serve is the most important stroke in tennis. It is the only shot in the game that is not a return of a shot hit by your opponent. As you stand at the baseline ready to serve, you are in complete control of the point, and how well you hit that serve will determine, to a large extent, how the point will go.

Some players have won major championships solely on the strength of their service. A five-star example is Bob Falkenburg, who won the Wimbledon singles title in 1948. Bob's game had obvious weaknesses, but his serve was so overwhelming he rarely lost it. It was a tremendous psychological weapon too. I know I spent a lot of sleepless hours wondering how to return that immensely powerful delivery that skidded so fast on grass.

I will now proceed to tell you how to serve just like Bob Falkenburg, so that you, too, can win the Wimbledon singles title. Dream on. What I do hope to show you, whether you are a beginner or a veteran, is how to develop an effective serve so that at least you can beat your favorite opponent.

Let's start with beginners. If you have never served before, I want you to concentrate on a simple, effortless swing, putting the ball into play with a flat serve. I should mention right here that in topflight tournament tennis there is no such thing as a completely flat serve. All serves, including

12

the so-called "cannonball," are hit with at least some spin on the ball for control. Even Pancho Gonzales, who hits the hardest serve in the game, puts a bit of spin on his big serve. If Pancho doesn't hit a completely flat serve, why should you, a beginner? Because, unlike Gonzales, you won't be hitting the ball hard enough to have a control problem, and until you have learned the fundamental serving motion I don't want you fooling around with spins.

For the flat serve, use the eastern forehand grip, which you assume by taking the throat of the racket in your left hand and shaking hands with the handle with your right. (This is a right-handed world, and left-handers, as usual, will have to adjust accordingly.) This grip allows you to hit the ball easily with a forward motion of the arm, getting the full face of the racket into the ball.

Taking your stance at the baseline, you should position yourself about 2 feet to the left or right of the center mark, depending on which court you are serving to. Your

Figure 3.

Proper Stance.

A

B

C

left foot, pointing at a 45° angle to the baseline, should be 2 or 3 inches behind it to avoid the possibility of a foot fault. Your right foot should be perhaps 18 inches behind the left and almost parallel to the baseline. Above all, you should feel comfortable.

Now you are ready to toss the ball into the air, an important step. Ideally, it would be best to hang the ball from a skyhook and suspend it at the proper height—as high as you can reach with your racket above your head. Skyhooks being illegal in tennis, you have to toss the ball up there. To insure accuracy, keep the left elbow close to the body, the left forearm parallel to the ground. Hold the ball lightly in the fingertips, palm up, and, in a smooth motion, raise your arm and release the ball. Do not make the mistake some people do and release the ball at shoulder level, and do not let go of it abruptly as if the ball were on fire. There's no hurry.

The toss itself should be just high enough to reach the hitting zone, which is where the racket is when you extend your arm overhead. You want to hit the ball at that precise moment between its rise and fall when it is not moving. If you toss the ball too high—and this is a common error—it will be descending rapidly when you attempt to hit it, presenting you with an additional timing problem. If you do not toss the ball high enough, you will lose that desirable combination of leverage and angle that enables you to hit the service hard across the net yet down into the service court. The higher your racket makes contact with the ball, the more service-court area you have for a target.

So much for height. What about direction? The toss should be about an arm's length in front of you, that is, toward the net. You want to hit the ball as your body is moving toward the net in order to get more power behind your serve. If your toss goes up directly overhead, you will have to lean back to hit the ball, if you *can* hit it.

If you have always had trouble controlling the ball when you toss it, try holding only one ball when you serve. You are allowed two serves in tennis, but there is no rule that says you must hold both balls at the same time. If your hand is small, put the second ball in your pocket. Women who wear tennis dresses can sew on a pocket and start a new fashion.

Another thought: If you do make a poor toss, one that promises to land 5 feet behind you, let the ball drop. You don't have to hit every ball you toss. Granted, it is not etiquette to make five tosses for every serve, but once in a while it is all right.

Now we come to the business end of the serve, the actual swing. Essentially, the service stroke is a throwing motion. The difference between Willie Mays throwing to the plate and Pancho Gonzales serving an ace is very slight. Pretend your racket is a ball and "throw" it a few times. That's the motion of the serve. What you are doing when you serve is throwing your racket across the net. If, when you hit a serve, you were to let go of your racket, it should land in the general area of your opponent's service court.

A Union of Two Motions

The service requires the coordination of two separate activities aimed at bringing the ball and racket into perfect union at the top of the swing. First, you should take your position about 4 or 5 feet from the center of the baseline, allowing you to either hit down the middle or angle the serve across court. Your weight is evenly distributed on your two feet. The racket is tilted at a slight upward angle with the throat cradled gently in the fingers of your left hand. The balls should be held comfortably in your fingers, not in the palm. Relaxation and balance are the most important keys to the stance at this particular moment.

The stroke begins with both arms commencing their separate actions simultaneously. The right (serving) arm moves back like a pendulum, the wrist remaining in a natural, uncocked position until the racket is overhead and behind your back, your weight shifting to your rear foot.

When your elbow has reached the height of your shoulder in this continuous, circular backswing, the wrist is broken and the racket head drops. Then the forward thrust begins. Make your toss as your racket comes around, shift your weight forward and keep your eye on the ball. As the wrist snaps the racket head forward, you achieve the feel of "throwing" the racket—just as if it were a baseball—across the net and into the service court for which you are aiming. The follow-through is natural. Once the ball has been struck, the right foot follows across the baseline in the direction the ball is taking, thus returning you to the anticipatory position from which you are ready to begin the next stroke.

Timing is important: The left arm throws the ball in a natural, easy motion—the racket must meet it at the absolute top of the toss, with the ball neither rising nor falling at the point of impact. This requires intensive practice, inasmuch as the toss must instinctively place the ball where the racket will strike it at a maximum height without overreaching.

Just as a pitcher needs more than a fast ball to be effective, you should add some variety to your service once you have learned to control the flat serve—*repeat*—when you have learned to control the flat serve. A pitcher has to throw strikes, and you have to put the ball into play. Unless you can do that, there is no game.

To put spin on your serve, use the backhand grip. Assume your normal forehand grip and move your hand an eighth of a turn to the left: instant backhand grip. This will make it easier for your wrist to snap the racket across the face of the ball.

The stance and toss are the same as before, but the motion of the racket is now part forward and part sideways. Whereas you hit the ball solidly before, you are now going to slice across it. Imagine the ball as the face of a clock. When you hit the flat serve, you hit dead center, the spot where the two hands of a clock are joined. Now, to put a spin on your serve, you bring the racket across the face of the

Figure 4. The Serve.

At the start, the racket is cradled in the left hand, right elbow close, weight on back foot (A). The toss begins with a racket backswing. Then start to shift weight forward as racket reaches the bottom of the swing (B).

(continued)

Body coil builds up power (C). As forward motion starts, the ball approaches the peak (D). The toss must be accurate with the body thrown forward, the ball met at full extension of the racket and the arm approximately 24 inches in front of the baseline (E). The left arm serves as a good counterbalance.

E

F

Snap your wrist forward pointing the racket head toward the receiving court (F), shifting your weight to the left foot, which pivots only slightly throughout.

(continued)

G

H

Thereupon the right foot is pulled naturally forward, bringing the body back to the anticipatory position (G and H).

ball and hit slightly to the right of center. This will send the ball into the court with a slight right-to-left spinning movement. Of course, the first time you try it you may hit too much of the ball or not enough, and you may even hit the ball on the edge of the frame—a home run in any park. But practice should iron out most of these flaws. In time you will find that you have more control over the spin than over a hard, straight serve.

Once you master the basic spin, a whole new world awaits you if you are willing to experiment and practice. You can hit your serve hard—your cannonball—and yet control it by hitting the ball just right of dead center. By tossing the ball slightly more to the right and—remember the face of the clock—hitting the ball at 3 o'clock, you can produce a truly wicked slice that goes screaming in low over the net.

You can also hit an American twist. Same grip, same stance. The toss, too, is essentially the same, except that you want the ball closer to you, almost directly overhead.

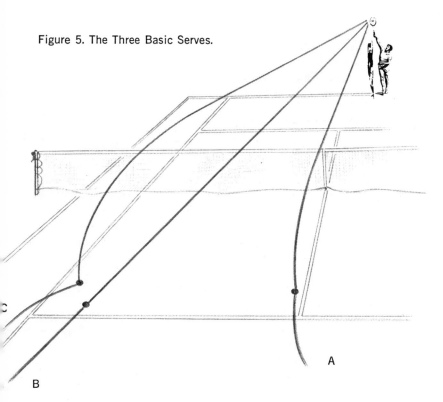

Figure 5. The Three Basic Serves.

From their point of origin—the racket—the slice, the cannonball and the American twist follow widely separate paths. The slice (A) crosses the net low, curving to the opponent's right. The cannonball (B) comes in faster and almost straight. The twist (C) clears the net and, when hit close to the doubles alley, kicks left, forcing the opponent off court.

You must arch your back, bring the racket farther behind your head and hit the ball where 10 or 11 o'clock would be. Again, as in the basic spin, your wrist does the work, for it is the snap of the wrist that puts the spin in motion. The action on the ball should make it clear the net by a safe margin and then drop sharply into the court. When it does, it should kick high to your opponent's left, his backhand side if he is right-handed, and, unless your opponent is named Budge, this is a plus.

It is not enough just to put the ball into the court, of course. A service court is 13½ feet by 21 feet deep, and you should use as much of that area as you can. A serve to the back corner of the court is obviously going to be more difficult for your opponent to return than a serve that is down the middle and only medium deep. Sure, once in a while you can surprise an opponent by hitting the ball directly at him but, as with the strike zone in baseball, the corners are where you want to put the ball. When you practice serving, try placing a couple of empty ball cans in the corners of the service court and then see if you can knock them down. Having a target to aim at will increase your accuracy and relieve some of the drudgery of practice.

Try to get your first serve in, even if it means letting up on it a little. There are several reasons for this. When you hit a fault, it gives your opponent a lift, a little edge. He also will probably move up a bit for your second serve. Don't give him that lift or the better court position. Pop that first ball right in there and wear him out. Of course, you can't let up on your serve too much or you'll defeat your purpose. There's a third reason for putting in your first serve. Tennis has become a battle for the net, and to get yourself into volleying position you must start your forward motion the instant you hit your serve. If that first serve is a fault, you have wasted energy. In the course of three sets or so this extra movement can be taxing.

There are such things as beautiful days for tennis—not too warm or bright and no wind—but never when I play.

Or so it seems. Whenever I go to serve, an Arabian sun is glaring down directly into my eyes. Sunglasses or a cap with a visor helps, but usually I find the best solution is to adjust my toss ahead, behind or even slightly below the sun.

Fast court surfaces—grass, wood, cement—are a good server's delight. On these, the cannonball is tough to return, for the ball will skid rather than bounce. On slower surfaces —clay, asphalt, composition—don't knock yourself out trying for aces. Concentrate on accuracy.

Now you are on your own. How you serve—grip, stance, toss and swing—is largely an individual matter. I have drawn rough guidelines, but the rest is up to you. You must practice and, as you do, feel free to experiment. If your grip does not feel quite right, shift it a fraction. If your feet do not feel comfortable, move them. Be flexible. And most important of all during all this trial and error and practice, don't forget to have fun.

THE FOREHAND

The workhorse of tennis is the forehand drive, the staple of the game for most players. It can be the big stick with which to beat down your opponent or the last bulwark of defense when all else fails. The best forehand is the simplest, and none proves the point better than Budge's. When Don hits the shot it is a free and effortless movement, a fluid sweep with the arm and racket as one.

The forehand and the backhand—the so-called ground strokes of tennis—are useful in direct proportion to their pace, depth and accuracy. Pace and depth come only from the perfect blending of those magic ingredients of any good athletic stroke—coordination and timing; in other words, the ability to lean your weight and strength into the shot at the exact moment you strike the ball. Accuracy and the ability to place the ball you will learn by subtle shifts in the distribution of your weight. It is about evenly divided

23

between your two feet on shots down the right sideline; on cross-court shots it is shifted to the left foot somewhat sooner.

One added point on ground strokes: Never neglect the follow-through. Hit the ball with confidence and decision and always *finish the shot*.

Two Perfect Arcs

On the forehand, each arm should describe a perfect arc in the course of the stroke. The left arm follows the right arm into the hitting position and starts the racket head on

Figure 6. The Forehand.

its backward motion before turning the work load over to the right. As the right arm takes over, it completes the backswing with the racket head high. Then the right shoulder drops, guiding the racket into the bottom of the arc just before it meets the ball. As contact is made, the full force of the racket is brought across the lower inside of the ball. The wrist is cocked until point of contact, when it locks with the forearm to utilize full power. The left arm swings forward and around in front of the body. The stroke is always completed with a full follow-through.

Start moving from the anticipatory position (A) as soon as you sense the direction of the oncoming ball. Never taking your eye off the ball, pivot on your right foot and cross over with the left, keeping your body sideways to net (B). Put your entire weight on your back foot and counterbalance with your left arm (C). The racket head continues back, reaching the top part of the arc, the face of the racket still open (D).

C

D

(continued)

E

F

The elbow and arm straighten as the racket head travels below the ball and the weight transfers to your left foot. Left arm leads forward thrust (E). Note the fluid body motion. The finish of the shot finds the racket head slightly above shoulder level to give free and confident follow-through (H). The weight remains forward as the arm and racket action pull the right side around to the anticipatory position and the left hand resumes its hold on the racket. A firm wrist propels the racket forward, your full body weight leaning in, the racket head below the wrist, your elbow away from your body (F). With your arm fully extended, hit the ball comfortably about 18 inches in front of the left foot (G). Always keep your eyes fixed on the ball.

THE BACKHAND

The backhand drive is executed on the same mechanical principle as the forehand drive. Properly hit, it can be just as effective as the forehand. The average player finds the backhand shot more difficult than the forehand, but actually it should be easier because you're swinging away from your body. Contrary to general belief, it should be an attacking and not a defensive weapon.

Budge's backhand, the strongest shot in his repertoire, is a classic stroke without an ounce of lost motion. In Figure 7, note especially his perfect weight distribution—from the left to right—and his free and easy follow-through. A good rule is to get as close to your work as possible without cramping so as to meet the ball comfortably in the center of the racket head. You should never be so far from the ball that you feel you have to make an undue effort to reach it. Note also how the elbow, as in the forehand stroke, is held close to the body until forward motion starts—then straightens to release coiled energy.

The left arm is unusually important to a good backhand. To start with, it does most of the work in taking the racket back to the start-forward position. From this point it serves an equally vital function in helping achieve and maintain balance. An interesting and sound formula to follow is that of executing a perfect circle in preparing for and completing the shot. Wait for the shot from the squared position (always on your toes), pivot, swing, follow through and return to the original position, waiting for the next shot.

The Perfect Circle

The backhand must be a fluid and continuous motion, not a series of separate acts performed one after the other.

28

Figure 7. The Backhand.

In the anticipatory position (A) you are facing the net, on your toes for quick movement, with the racket held easily in both hands, elbows in close. Then pivot on the left foot (B) as the left arm pulls the racket and torso back.

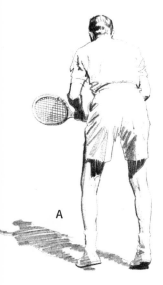

A

B

(continued)

Properly executed, the steps are simple and related, creating a natural sequence without hesitation or acceleration. Starting with the anticipatory position in the backcourt, the right hand is relaxed on the handle, the throat of the racket cradled lightly in the left. As the ball approaches, you move into position, following the flight of the ball. That is of the utmost importance. The left hand guides the racket until

Body pivot (C) comes next, stepping over with your right foot so your back is half turned to net. The right hand makes a quarter turn to left for a grip change and receives the work load as the racket head reaches the highest point of arc (D) and is about to drop into position (E). The racket head starts below the flight of the ball, the right shoulder well down (F).

C

D

the downward arc begins, when the right hand tightens its grip. At point of contact—approximately 12 inches in front of the right foot—the ball should be met waist high. If the bounce is low, the knees should be bent more to meet the ball at its height. The shot should be made with a firm grip, the wrist straightening and locking naturally at the time of contact.

F

E

(continued)

The right arm is straightened and brought around the body. Hit into and straight through (G), transferring your weight from the left leg to the right. Naturally following through, the racket ends at shoulder level or slightly higher (H). The body remains collected yet relaxed, leaning into the stroke. The left arm counterbalances and permits a full and easy follow-through motion (G and H). The last step is a pivot on the right foot (I) to bring your feet, knees, hips, shoulders, head, eyes, arms and racket back to anticipatory position (A). The circle of action is then complete.

Figure 8. Baseball Swing Analogy.

Baseball swing is the analogy Budge used to describe backhand motion. He likened it to the swing of Ted Williams.

A WAY TO BETTER NET PLAY

You have been invited to play doubles with friends, and the moment has arrived when your partner is about to serve and you must play net. Of course, there is no tennis law that insists you have to play net, but you should want to. Tennis, even at club level, has become a serve-and-volley game and, in doubles especially, the team that controls the net generally will win.

33

The Grip

So there you are, up at the net. The first thing you should do is choose a grip. Take the throat of your racket in your left hand and with your right shake hands with the handle. This is the forehand grip. (See Figure 1, page 11.) Move the hand an eighth of a turn to the left and you have the backhand grip. (See Figure 2, page 11.) Most top players—Gonzales, Kramer, Budge—use a backhand grip when they volley. A few others prefer the forehand. Either is perfectly correct, and you should settle on the one that feels most comfortable. The important thing is to use only one grip when you volley. Hit your forehand and backhand volleys with the same grip. At net you simply do not have time to switch from one grip to another, as you do when you are hitting from the backcourt. Too often players try to switch grips, which explains why so many of their volleys go straight up, straight down—just about anywhere except over the net into the other court. It may feel a little awkward at first, hitting a forehand volley with a backhand grip, but you will get used to it and be better off doing it.

The Stance

I shudder every time I see a player standing at the net, arms at his sides, racket pointing down. No wonder he is beaten so often by easy shots. You must be ready up there. You should hold the racket right out in front of you so that the tip of it is pointing straight ahead. Keep your left hand at the throat of the racket for balance. This way you will be able to move the racket as quickly as possible.

It is also important to keep mentally alert. The best way I know of doing this is to expect every shot to be yours. Think: "This shot is coming at me." If it does not, no harm done. If it does, you will be ready. There is no reason why you should not be alert at the net.

The Volley

And so, alert, racket up, grip set, you await the start of the point. Your partner serves, and your opponent hits his return—right at you. Well, at least you were expecting it, so you are not surprised. Now, if you have never played net, or if you have played it only when ordered to, chances are you will stand aside and let your partner take it, if he can. This, of course, is a mistake. If you have always enjoyed playing net but usually have missed more shots than you have made, chances are you will take a healthy swing at the ball. This is also a mistake. Do not swing at the ball when you volley. Balls hit at you at the net generally have so much speed that all you need do is block them. If the opponent's shot is weak, you can add a little punch to your volley, like a boxer's jab. Keep your wrist locked and jab, but do not take a backswing. Oh, if your opponent should hit a real lollipop over the net, swing ahead and have fun. But if you insist on swinging at fast shots which are coming at you from close range, your chances of hitting the ball where you want it to go are small. Most likely you will be late, like a batter swinging at a good fast ball. By blocking the ball your racket will have become, in effect, a tennis backboard, and backboards fail to return very few shots.

You may argue at this point—especially if you have never played net—that your reflexes are not nearly quick enough to make volleys, to block off a fast shot hit at point-blank range. It is true that some people have quicker reflexes than others, but just about everyone can react fast enough to play net. Have you ever seen a player duck out of the way of a shot hit, say, right at his chin? The shot, he thinks, came at him too fast to hit, and he considers himself lucky to have moved his head while he still had it. But if he had enough time to move his head he probably had enough time to volley the ball. Chances are he was not

Figure 9. The Volley.

Short punch characterizes the backhand volley as well as the forehand. With the racket head held slightly above your locked wrist, the racket travels about 12 to 18 inches as you take a short step into the ball. The angle of the racket head is increased with lower shots.

Figure 10. Another Baseball Analogy.

Start the volley with the racket head where the mitt would be if you were catching a baseball. Then, taking a short forward step with the left foot, use the arm and racket as one lever to make a short, sharp movement into the oncoming ball. The best volleyers are those who confine themselves to the essential motions of the shot and thus minimize the area in which they operate. When hitting a volley at about the level of the net cord, snap the wrist; lower volleys must be played with the wrist locked.

expecting the shot, and when it came he panicked and ducked.

Panic is not an unnatural feeling at the net. A good way to overcome it is to have someone toss balls at you, slowly at first, but with increasing speed. When it is no longer foreign to you to have a ball coming at you, you will feel more at ease.

Of course, not every shot will come directly at you. Suppose one of your opponents hits a shot wide of you, get within range of your outstretched arm. Faced with this situation, too many players simply reach out like a first baseman stretching for a wide throw and volley the ball for better or worse. Usually worse. In tennis there is no bag to keep your foot on, and there is no need to act as though there is. You should step into the ball. If you can volley the ball at close range—say, a foot or two from your body—you will have much better control in making the shot.

Along similar lines, if you have to volley a ball that has fallen below the level of the net, you must get down to it. Bend the knees, crouch. You cannot expect to make an effective volley of a low ball standing stiff-legged. Incidentally, you should always try to get to the ball while it is above the level of the net. You want to volley the ball down and make the opponents hit the ball up. That is what tennis is all about. It is a cardinal sin to let a ball drop when you might have hit it sooner.

The Overhead

The overhead is an essential part of the net game, for as soon as you have shown you can volley well, your opponents will stop trying to hit the ball past you and start trying to lob it over you. Unless you can return these lobs with overheads, your entire net game will suffer.

The overhead swing should be short and lethal; I like to compare it to hammering a nail in a wall just over your head. You do not wind up and clout the nail, because chances are good you will miss. And you will miss the ball if you try to hit it the same way. The shorter the swing, the less room there is for error. But don't forget to hit the ball and hit it hard, arm fully extended at the point of contact.

Nor should your feet leave the ground when you hit an overhead, except when absolutely necessary. If you learn to get back quickly, it should not be necessary to jump often.

Lastly, do not be overly concerned where you hit your overhead. More overheads are missed because the player was trying to check the last-second movements of the opponents. Forget that sort of thing and simply hit the ball.

Positioning

I have not discussed where you should stand at the net because so much depends on how effective your volleying and your overhead are. I recently played tennis against a good player who was not very tall but who insisted on crowding the net. Now, it is a distinct advantage to play close to the net, because you can get more of a downward angle on your volleys, but this only applies if you are tall enough, or quick enough, to handle the lob. This fellow I was playing against was not. His partner would serve and charge the net, and it was the easiest thing in the world to lob over them. They would have to run back and we would be at the net. If he had been my partner I would have said: "Look, move back a couple of steps. You just don't have the overhead to play that close."

In general, I would say the proper place to play when your partner is serving or when your partner is receiving serve is about 2 yards inside the service line and a couple of feet inside the doubles alley. But position must remain a flexible thing, depending on your ability, the ability of your opponents and how the match is going.

Poaching

When you have learned how to volley, you should practice it often in matches. A good volleyer can dominate an otherwise even game, but only if he is aggressive. If you allow a steady stream of service returns to float back across the middle of the net, many of which lead to points for the opponents, you have yourself to blame. You should be cutting off those shots at the net—if not all of them, at least some. This is called poaching, and not enough players practice it.

Poaching requires good timing. If you start moving across

39

the court too soon, your opponent will hit the ball behind you down the alley. If you leave too late—well, you are too late. You must wait until the moment that your opponent commits himself to his shot. It is very much like the steal in baseball. As a matter of fact, I have played a lot of tennis with Jackie Robinson and, as you can imagine, Jackie is an excellent poacher.

Always keep alert to the tide of battle during a point. If, for instance, your partner has laced a return at the feet of your opponent, be prepared to poach. That opponent must hit the ball up to clear the net, a weak shot, a shot you should try to put away. But if your opponent is about to volley a ball from the height of his shoulders, better hold your ground, for he will be hitting the ball down, an attacking shot.

Poaching accomplishes two things. If successful, it wins points, abruptly. Secondly, it rattles the opponent. Knowing that the net man likes to poach puts the opponent under pressure. Is he going to cross this time? Should I try to hit it down his alley? Thoughts like these can make an inexperienced player hit shots everywhere but in the court. It can even bother experienced players.

When I was captain of the U.S. Davis Cup team in 1953, it was pretty clear that a crucial match would be the doubles. I had Tony Trabert and Vic Seixas. The Australians were going to use Lew Hoad and Rex Hartwig, and they were, on the record, a better team than our boys. I felt we had to do something to upset them, so I tried an old system Gardnar Mulloy and I had often used. Just before one of our players was to serve, the other would turn his back to Hoad and Hartwig and signal whether or not he was about to poach. That way the server would know and could cover up for his partner—that is, rush the net on the side of the court his poaching partner had just vacated. But the real value of this signal system is that it created a psychological barrier for Hoad and Hartwig. It gave them something to worry about. Trabert and Seixas won in straight sets.

Equally disconcerting to opponents is the fake poach. To lean on baseball again, the fake poach is similar to Maury Wills taking a long lead from first base, breaking toward second with the pitch and stopping after three steps. The last thing the pitcher sees as he turns his head toward the plate is Wills streaking toward second, and this cannot help his pitching. Faking a poach is equally distracting to a man returning a serve. Seeing you break early, he may try to hit the ball behind you, in which case you will be right there waiting for it. Even if he hits the ball cross-court, chances are it will not be a good shot.

Court Manners

Let me stress that there is nothing unethical or unsportsmanlike about poaching or faking a poach. You should use all the little tricks you can. Above all, if the opponents are having success with a certain pattern of play, you should employ any legitimate tactic to disrupt that pattern. You may continue to lose, but at least you will not be losing the same way.

There are, however, questions of taste in tennis. In a friendly game you can poach too much and spoil everyone's game. It isn't any fun playing with someone who poaches on every shot, or who is always trying complicated shots. I agree that it's great to try a crazy shot—a difficult lob volley or an impossibly sharp angle—but not on every shot. It's nice to win, and a strong net game will help you win, but the main point is for all players to have fun.

THE LEFT HAND IN THE GAME OF TENNIS

When the Creator laid out the blueprint for man's anatomy. he gave him, among other things, two hands. He must have deemed that both hands have a purpose.

In some sports, one hand is used more than the other, but both hands have vital functions in every sport. They work together. They coordinate. They supplement each other. This is as true in tennis—where the left arm and hand often appear to be a loose, swinging and useless appendage— as in golf, baseball and basketball.

In golf, the left hand is the controlling hand. It grips and swings the club. The right hand, overlapping lightly, serves mainly as a guide or part of a hinge. Thus, natural left-handers, such as Ben Hogan, have become great golfers by switching to a right-hand stance. They provide natural strength to the side that's needed.

In baseball, both hands grip the bat. In the field, one hand wears the glove and the other is left free to throw—a different function. In basketball, both hands are equally important on defense. On offense, the ball may be passed or projected goalward by both hands, or by one—either one. In the case of a one-handed shot, the other hand supports the ball, steadies it.

But the left hand is the forgotten hand of tennis. Most of us never think about it unless it be in the discussion of natural left-hand players such as the great Rod Laver. But we are discussing here the important function of the left hand for the right-hand player. If you're a left-hander, this analysis is reversed. The right hand becomes the odd—or loose—hand.

The importance of the left hand in tennis is brought sharply into focus before the first ball is struck. It comes in the service. The left hand throws up the ball. No matter how fluid or how powerful is the service stroke, it cannot succeed if there is a faulty toss.

The ball should be thrown slightly in front of the server and at the exact height of the racket in full overhead stretch. It should be hit at the apex of its loft. Thus timing—the meeting of the ball and the racket at the exact instance and at the proper height—determines the effective service. The left hand provides the key, the right hand the power.

Once the ball has been put into play, the competitor may feel that now—for all it's worth—the left arm could be chopped off at the shoulder and discarded until time for the next service. Nothing is further from the truth. The left hand has a very critical function in helping keep the racket in position between strokes. After a ball has been hit, the racket should be returned to the body and nestled in the left hand.

The left hand should hold the racket at the throat. This takes pressure off the right hand, which would undergo

Figure 11. The Anticipatory Position.

This is your position of security to which you return after every shot. The body, well relaxed, is poised on the toes, weight forward. The racket is cradled in the left hand, ready for the next shot.

tremendous strain and certainly would tend to tire without this support. With the racket held in this ready position across the front of the body—the right hand resting gently on the handle, the left supporting it at the throat—the

Figure 12.

A. Forehand.

B. Backhand.

player is in position to move quickly either to the right or left, depending on the return.

Actually, the two-handed ready position during play has an added value, which must be credited to the ledger of the left hand. It forces the body turn on the forehand and backhand. For the well-hit ground stroke, the racket should be brought back with both hands—the left still on the throat, forcing the essential turn of the body. With the racket now ready to go forward, the job is turned over to the right side.

Youngsters beginning tennis at an early age often have trouble getting the racket around—especially off the backhand—with one hand. So they improvise by using a two-handed, or baseball, grip, affording them additional power. It is a habit some players—and very good ones—never lose.

One of the most prominent of these is Cliff Drysdale, the brilliant South African. He has retained the two-fisted backhand and it is his most effective weapon, the ball coming off his racket like a cannon shot. The veteran Ecuadorian professional, Pancho Segura, now head instructor at the fashionable LaCosta Country Club in California, uses a two-fisted forehand with equal devastation. Beverly Baker Fleitz, former national public parks champion and a Top Ten player in the 1950's, also used a two-handed backhand stroke. Although these three have been very successful, I wouldn't recommend the two-fisted shot under any circumstances. It reduces a player's reach considerably.

The left hand has still another use for the right-hand player. It not only helps in forcing the body-turn shot but also helps in adjusting the grip. Most players make a slight shift of the grip before hitting the backhand stroke. (See Figure 7d, page 30.) If there were not a left hand to make this constant adjustment—instantaneously in a fast game—it would be necessary to flip the racket in the air and attempt to capture the proper grip in flight. This is not only awkward but virtually impossible for most players. The good volleyer uses the left hand to get the racket into position

45

quickly. It is a tremendous aid in getting the racket in the ready position.

Tennis is a difficult game to master at best. The job is easier if one uses all the facilities available. One of the most important of these is the left hand. Don't forget you've got it.

THE STRATEGIES OF SINGLES

To be genuinely helpful, a tennis book should be concerned not only with *how to play* the game but *how to win*. What, for example, is the actual advantage in points won of the big-serve-and-volley game? How important statistically is the first serve? The second? The return? What is the most effective target for a passing shot? A kill?

The world's best tennis players, going all out to win in game after game at Forest Hills, Wimbledon, River Oaks, Paris and elsewhere, provided some of the answers. They reported, for instance, that the first serve accounts for 33 per cent of all winning strokes in the modern game. More important, perhaps, 50 per cent of all first serves are aimed at the outside corners of the service courts (A in Diagram 1). Second serves, on the other hand, are more likely to be hit to the receiver's backhand in both service courts (A in Diagram 2) and when thus aimed are about as effective in winning points as the harder-hit first serves. Returns of service were, of course, less easy to plot and analyze, but an index of their importance is the fact that some 25 per cent of serves are not returned at all.

Obviously, no set of diagrams could cover every contingency in a game where an attack can be met by a dozen different defenses, any one of which in turn opens the door to new attacks. On pages 47–52, six classic situations are diagrammed. Straight lines indicate the flight paths of stroked balls; the dash-dot line is a lob. Ovals show positions of players; dashed lines, their movements. A careful study of these situations will give every player, whether weekend or tournament, a better understanding of the strategic and tactical nature of tennis.

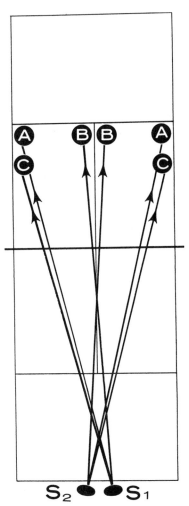

Diagram 1. Aim Points for First Serves.

The preferred aim points for first serves are in order of preference A, B, C. Serves to the forehand court are made from S_1, and serves to the backhand court from S_2. The favorite aim point (A), used in at least half the cases, is deep to the outside corner. The purpose is to force the receiver far out of position, opening up the whole court for a winning first volley by the server. Aim points B and C are used to keep the receiver guessing, to capitalize on a stroke weakness of his or to take advantage of his being out of proper receiving position.

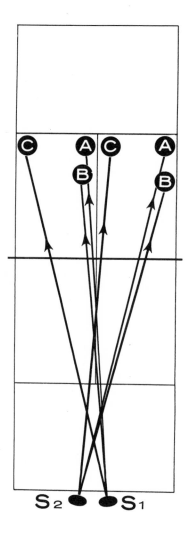

Diagram 2. Aim Points for Second Serves.

On second serves, the preferred aim is to the same areas in both service courts. The American twist is almost invariably used for the second serve because (1) it is easy to control, cutting down on double faults; (2) its slower speed gives the server enough time to get well into the net; and (3) its high-bounding kick to the backhand is one of the most difficult balls for the average receiver to return effectively. Since it naturally spins the ball to areas A and B, two-thirds of the serves in the forehand court and three-fourths of those in the backhand fall into these areas. Serves sliced to area C and its vicinity are designed only to keep the receiver guessing.

Diagram 3. Aim Points for
Return of Deep Service
Against Net-Rushing Server.

On first and second serves hit deep
to area 1 in the forehand court, the
experts return some 40 per cent
cross court to aim point A, 40 per
cent to the middle (aim point B),
and 20 per cent down the line to
aim points C or D.

From area 3 the cross-court return
to aim point A gives more outright
winners. Most returns from area 2
are hit back to aim point B. On the
matter of over-all won and lost, the
cross-court and down-the-line returns are almost equally effective—
about 55 per cent of successful returns to these areas resulting in
points won. Of returns to the middle
(aim point B), only 40 per cent result in points won.

This means that on deep serves
to the forehand court the receiver
should try to direct his return down-
the-line or cross court as shown in
the diagram. Either one forces the
server to advance further to reach
for the volley, thus causing him to
make errors, or weak volleys which
present the receiver with opportuni-
ties to make successful passing
shots. On the other hand, the return
to the middle can usually be volleyed by the server less hurriedly
and more effectively.

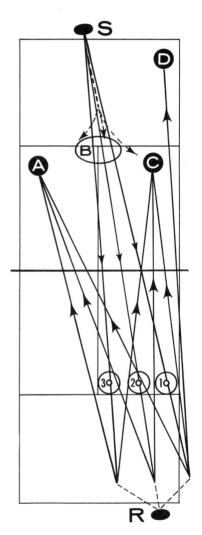

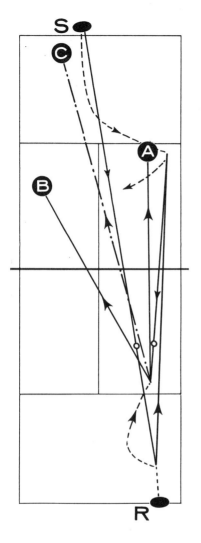

Diagram 4. A Good Passing Shot.

A good passing shot depends on the ability of the passer to force his opponent into volleying short—within a few feet of the service line at the maximum. You win more points by drawing an error from the volleyer by making him reach than you do by executing a clean pass. On very short balls it is often best to hit the passing shot right at the crest of the volleyer to draw an error.

Here, for example, receiver R moves in and hits the return early and low down the line. This catches server S near the service line and forces him to reach far to his left to make the volley from near the ground. The receiver should anticipate a volley hit up weakly and in a down-the-line direction. There is practically nothing else the server can do. Thus, the receiver should move in a bit and get set to capitalize on the short volley, as shown. He must watch the server as well as the ball. If the server starts to move to the center, the passing shot can be chipped safely down the line to aim point A. And if the server is slow to recover, the receiver has a wide-open court to hit a slightly-topped passing shot cross court—with room to spare—to aim point B. If the server moves in close to the net to try to cut off either return, an offensive lob can be dumped neatly over his head to aim point C.

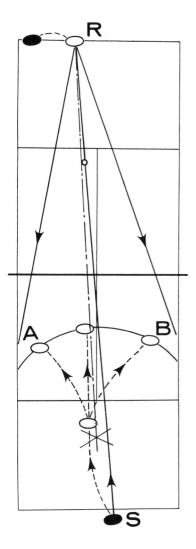

Diagram 5. Going to Net.

Going to net behind the serve, the server must in general follow a line bisecting the angle (ARB). As shown here in a serve down the middle to the forehand court, the server's best position is a few inches on the receiver's forehand side of that bisector, since the return probably will be slightly faster on that side. Note that as the server comes closer in to the net, the space between the AR and BR lines narrows. He thus has less ground to cover. A driven return off a fast service seldom gives the server enough time to get in much closer than a step inside the service line. However, the server has a chance to cover such shots, because a hard drive cannot be hit at a wide angle along lines AR and RB, as it will sail over the sideline.

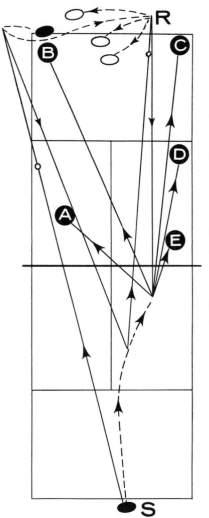

Diagram 6. Going for the Kill.

Going for the kill means hitting to a place where your opponent isn't or hitting behind him as he moves. Here server S is getting set to make his second volley and from watching his opponent he must decide in split seconds where to place it. If receiver R hesitates too long, server can volley a high ball to aim point A or, if the ball is low, deep to point B. If receiver commits himself to the left, however, a high ball can be slammed to point C, a low ball to point D or a drop volley to point E.

A ONE-TWO PUNCH FOR THE PRETTIEST

Girls playing tennis are prettier than anybody, but they are not necessarily more effective. Even the hardest-fought women's matches at country clubs from Newport, Rhode

Island, to Newport Beach, California, usually are ground-stroke duels marked by long, graceful rallies during which neither competitor is likely to approach the net or the backstop. This kind of tennis looks very pretty, and it's a fine way to catch a date for the Saturday dance from the gallery, but it's no good for winning matches against either men or other women.

A good many years ago, I was interested only in getting a date for the Saturday dance when I ran into an agitated blonde tennis player at a club in Ohio. But she was more interested in winning tennis. "Oh, Bill," she almost sobbed, "I'll actually die if Charlotte beats me in the club tournament this year. Can't you show me how to beat her?"

I saw no problem. "Stick with me, honey," I said, "and I'll make you a champ." At least, I thought, I might get a date when the tournament was over. For the next two weeks my friend (whom we will call Serena) and I held daily practice sessions on a court conveniently hidden from the clubhouse, developing some new strokes. On the Saturday afternoon of the women's finals, she unveiled them against Charlotte (which wasn't her name either) and won the tournament.

What were the strokes? A drop shot and a lob.

These are effective strokes in anybody's repertoire, and I had first learned their true value only a few months before, when I was matched against a player far more experienced than I. He was picked to win easily, so, being young and brash, I decided to alter things a bit. On his first four serves, I answered with a drop shot just over the net which brought him lunging and stumbling from the baseline. When he returned the ball successfully, I floated a lob over his head, sending him panting to the backstop. The result: I won the match 6–0, 6–1.

I can't pretend that strategy based on two strokes would sweep through the national championships, but I can practically guarantee—as, in fact, I did to Serena—that in run-of-the-country-club women's tennis it will produce a win-

53

ning game and, provided your opponent is not also reading this article, a club championship.

The drop shot has been called the whipped cream of the stroke menu. It is produced by the gentlest kiss of the racket on the ball, just enough to drop the ball over the net for a quick death. (See Diagram 7.) To give a drop the disguise and spin that make it most effective, you approach it just as you would a normal ground stroke. Then, a split second before impact, you turn the racket face under to impart backspin, relax your grip and tap the ball. The more backspin you use, the harder you can hit the ball but the more difficult it is to make the shot. The almost horizontal position of the racket in extreme backspin means that the slightest mistiming of the stroke will cause you to hit the wood.

For the best drop shot, a ball at waist height should be hit with the racket face tilted at about 30 degrees from the vertical. The follow-through is in a downward direction and can be as short as 1 foot.

There are two kinds of lob, both of which should be

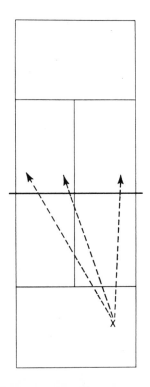

Diagram 7. The Drop Shot.

For a drop shot to be most effective, your opponent should be standing well back and you should hit the ball from inside the baseline (X in the diagram), aiming for placement right, left or center.

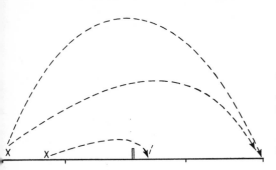

Diagram 8. Trajectories for the One-Two Punch.

The high arc is the defensive lob; the slightly flatter arc below it is the offensive lob. The lowest represents the drop shot.

mixed with the drop shot for a winning combination. (See Diagram 8.) The offensive lob can be hit either flat or with a slight topspin. I recommend the latter, because it bounces away from the player running back to retrieve it.

The defensive lob is best hit with an underspin. This serves two purposes: (1) it makes for better control, particularly in a wind, and (2) its backward rotation tends to slow the ball so that it hangs in the air to give the defensive lobber a chance to recover his position.

Many people think of a lob as no stroke at all, but merely a kind of push or shovel shot. It is no such thing. A good lob demands just as much precision as any other stroke. Because its greatest value lies in its disguise, it should be started off either side in the same way as the corresponding ground stroke. The only difference is in the angle of the racket face at the moment of impact and on the follow-through. In placing lobs, you should generally aim for the player's backhand area and as close to the baseline as you can get.

It takes practice to learn such placement, but when you have it and can use it in conjunction with the drop shot, you will have a one-two punch that will soon make a wreck of the steadiest backcourt duelist.

Try it out, girls, and I promise you'll all be club champions. But if you care to get invited to the Saturday dance, don't try it on your dates.

2
Doubles

DOUBLES, which mistakenly has been called singles in double harness, can be played by women as well as men and by people of all ages. Among the best tournament players, it is an extremely fast game requiring the ultimate in skill, ingenuity, reflexes and power. Among club players generally, it is a game of medium speed and moderate exertion. But for both groups it is surprisingly complicated. Partners who have studied its techniques and mastered its strategy can take on players of superior ability and condition and whip them so badly they will wonder why they bothered to play at all. That is the fascination—not to say devilish pleasure—of the game. Now to learn the fun of winning at doubles.

IT'S UP FRONT THAT COUNTS IN DOUBLES

Successful doubles, like successful warfare, is based on position, and the winning position in doubles is at the net, where an offense can be maintained. In games between skilled players, one out of every third shot is a volley and, excluding the service and return of service, 80 per cent of all points are won at the forecourt position. Similarly, 80 per cent of the placements in doubles are volleys. Thus, it

Figure 13.

A. Serving, a player is most effective if he has a consistent service that will force the receiver into a weak or defensive return. Partner stands 8 to 10 feet behind net, shaded slightly to the outside.

B. Following to net, the server moves rapidly to gain proper position for volleying. He should be in far enough to hit down for a placement or force a weak return that will lead to a winner. Volleying, the server should play his first return deep down middle, if the receiver hangs back. If he advances to the middle of the court, the return should be at his feet, where he will have no alternative but a shot from below the top of the net.

The server continues to advance to a position directly at his partner's side and in the middle of his side of the court. Thus positioned, both players can reach most returns hit over the net.

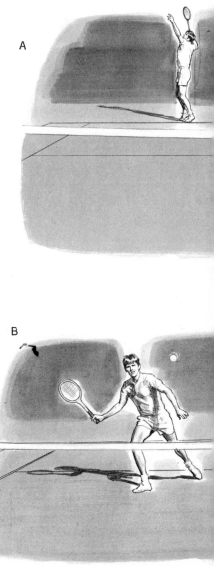

is imperative that both players concentrate on getting to the net and remaining there for every point. A player shall retreat to the base line only when he is forced back. Once driven there, he must wage a vigorous campaign to return to the net. On these pages you will learn how best to achieve the attacking position in doubles and how, as a result, to win.

MOVING LATERALLY FOR WIDEST NET COVERAGE

Against the majority of opposing strokes, the two basic positions shown in Figures 14 and 15 are the ones to strive for in net play. Generally, they should be returned to after each stroke, much as one returns to the center of the baseline in singles. The players' exact distance from the net should be determined by their heights, the speed of their reactions and their ability to anticipate the return.

A number of circumstances force a modification of the

Figure 14.

Covering center, partners concentrate on protecting the low part of the net, over which most shots will come. Net play depends to some degree on anticipating shots and moving quickly to the ideal position. But experienced partners know each other's playing habits, and often have a prearranged understanding about certain types of shots. It is important in doubles play to cover court width in order to prevent shots from being driven between teammates. However, when this is the case, the player not handling the shot must move swiftly to cover any section of the court exposed by his partner's action.

basic net position. A lob, for example, should make the net team drop back a step or so to prepare for an overhead smash. If the opponents are forced to hit up a weak shot, the net team should move closer to volley down or angle volley for a placement. The net team should practice shifting one man forward toward the center and the other back toward the sideline, the proper distance for each shift depending upon the angle from which the return is about to be made. The wider the opponents' angle, the better their chances of slipping by a passing shot.

Figure 15.

Offensive position at net should be practiced until it becomes second nature. Two men stationed approximately 8 feet from net and 12 feet apart can cover almost the complete width of net. When the opponents are stroking the ball from a wide angle, or from close in, the net players must shift relative positions to maintain court coverage. For instance, player at right in drawing below moves left to cover for partner. Movement is reversed if the ball is hit to the other side.

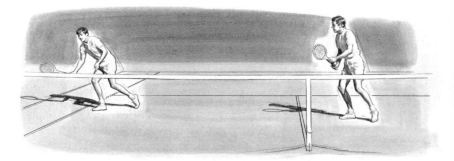

DEFENDING AGAINST THE SERVICE

The tactics of defense are directed toward the same end as those of offense—and that is to attack at the net as soon as possible. If the receiver can make an effective return of service and get well in to the net, he switches the odds on winning the point from two-to-one against him to two-to-one in his favor. A low, cross-court return, preferably not too fast, gives the receiving team the time it needs to reach the attacking position at the net. Another advantage of this kind of service return, which might better be named an approach shot, is that it cannot be volleyed down or through the receiver's partner. To keep the server and the net man guessing, an occasional flat drive cross court or down the line should be played by the receiver—or sometimes a lob might be tried. But, above all, the receiver must manage to get the ball back over the net, and by merely avoiding the outright loss of the point on the return of service, the receiving team assures itself an almost even chance of winning the point. A weak return over the net is much better than a spectacular error into it.

The vital area for the receiver is deep in his own backhand corner (1 and 2 in Diagram 9), where the server will try to place ball. Most serves are twists hit at about three-fourths speed. Using them, the server usually has greater control, better chance to get to the net. But the receiver must also be on the alert for other types of service and other speeds and targets which the server will resort to occasionally to prevent the receiver from taking liberties with the serve.

Wherever the ball is hit, the receiver's primary responsibility is to get it back, no matter how he has to hit it. "On a crucial point," Don Budge once said, speaking of his tournament days, "I always had only one thought: keep the ball in play." A return of service, it has been estimated, will result in winning the point 50 per cent of the time. The burden then rests on your opponents.

Figure 16.

Receiving serve, for best return a player should be a step inside the baseline. His partner should be at a modified net position just inside the service line and close to the center of his service court. Moving in after return, receiver should go as far toward net as he feels his shot justifies. If it is deep, he will have more time to get into position. At all times the return should make the opponent hit from below the top of the net.

Diagram 9.

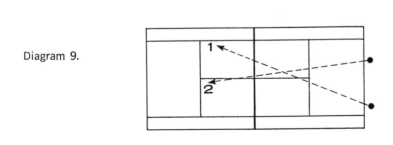

Figure 17.

A high lob is the best defense against a forcing serve and sometimes may be used to confuse opponents. It also gives the receiving team time to move to offense. If the serving team assumes a position very close to the net, the offensive lob is a good weapon.

THINKING IS HALF THE GAME

To be a winning combination, a team must realize that it can score as many points by outmaneuvering its opponents as it can with overpowering shots. Both players should concentrate fully on the game, however, and never permit themselves even the slightest mental lapses.

They must also be dedicated team men, and this does not imply the mere mechanical mastery of doubles techniques. Without good team morale, a wide repertoire of solid strokes and sound tactics cannot insure victory. Successful partners help one another with a steady exchange of encouragement, which not only wins points but, occasionally, saves points by settling down a ruffled player.

But it is the intelligent diagnosis of the opponents' game, finally, that makes the difference between a good team and an excellent one. Most players have a stroke weakness or a court-position weakness or both. A stroke weakness should be exploited by playing it, but not by *overplaying* it. Any weak stroke may become a strong weapon if you force the opponent to use it too much and thus promote his confidence in it. Similarly, a court-position weakness should be cashed in when needed, but not exploited to excess. A good doubles team will note carefully whether the opposing net man is too close to the net, or whether he leaves the alley or center unguarded. It

Figure 18.

Ready for return, the doubles pair inch up on the net, positioning themselves to get to the ball while it is still high, thereby assuring sharp, down-angled volley. However, since their position is very close to the net, they are vulnerable to an offensive lob.

will watch to see whether the opponents fail to move to the proper defensive position against a sharp cross-court return and whether returns of service are followed to the net. Once you have spotted such lapses, you can capitalize on them for crucial points.

THE DIFFICULT RETURN OF SERVICE

The return of service is the most difficult shot in doubles. This stroke more than any other determines how the point

Figure 19.

A high lob, forcing retreat to backcourt, should be taken by team member yelling "mine." He should smash if possible; the next best shot is a very high lob. If one partner has the better overhead, he should take as many shots as comfortably possible.

will go—and the serving team averages two points to every one for the receivers. Actually, 20 per cent of all attempted returns of service end up in errors, and only 12 per cent result in winners, a mere handful of which are placements.

The receiving team must get as close to an attacking position as possible. The partner of the receiver should be at a modified net position, just inside the service line and

Figure 20.

A serve deep in court should flatten out, not bounce up, to give the opponent attacking return. Ideally, the serving team should be able to follow serve to within 15 feet of the net, where defensive return can be put away.

near the center of the court. The receiver himself should be a step or more inside the baseline for a first service. Every step that is safe to move in against the particular server is an advantage, since it gives the receiver a better chance to take the serve early and return it offensively at the feet of the incoming server. It also saves the server more time to rush to the attacking position at the net.

FIVE RULES FOR DIVIDING THE COURT

Generally speaking, there are five basic rules to govern which return each of the partners should take. They are:

(1) A ball hit straight down center should be taken by the player with his forehand toward the center.

(2) A ball hit cross court should be taken by the man on the opposite side of the court from which the shot is made.

(3) A lob hit down the middle should be smashed by the man who can get to it with his forehand.

(4) During a rapid exchange at point-blank range, the man who last hits the ball should take shots returned down the center. It is usually easier for him to follow the ball and to anticipate the return.

(5) On a return of service hit down the center, the net man usually moves over to try to volley it away. However, the server must be prepared to back his partner up, should he fail to volley the ball.

68

USING SIGNALS TO VARY TACTICS

Once a doubles team is absolutely sure of its basic moves, it should work out variations that will keep its opponents off balance. Indeed, surprise changes are an important element in doubles play.

Everybody knows, for instance, that on the serve the man serving the ball stands on one side of the court and his partner stands on the other. But near the turn of the century some Americans and Australians experimented with a reverse formation for the serving team.

Hoping to offset the cross-court return of service, which often forced weak first volleys, they placed the net man on the same side of the court as the server. The trick worked well then and is still used to advantage today.

But it is not only on the serve that doubles partners should try unconventional formations. Using a variety of formations, poaches (that is, switching positions at the last possible instant and covering each other's territory) and fakes, a team can so upset its opponents that they will become more interested in what is going on in the opposite court than in following the ball. As a result, the opponents will fall into errors.

The tricky team, too, can err unless (1) it is sure of its basic moves and (2) it practices its deceptions. To avoid mistakes, partners should develop a set of signals to tell each other secretly what they will do. On many good doubles teams the net man is the person who gives the sign. Before play begins, he turns his back to the net, faces the server and then either flashes one or more fingers or holds his racket in such a way that the server—but no one else—knows exactly what to expect and where on the court he is supposed to move.

Such tactics not only give a team a variety of offenses and defenses, but they also present a psychological barrier to the opponents.

Figure 21.

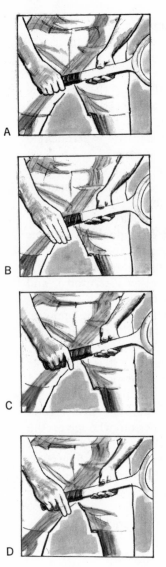

The full hand tells the server there will be no trick on upcoming serve. The signal is used to disconcert opponents, who, seeing the net man give signal, will be looking for a trick.

Four fingers tells the server the net man will poach on both serves to backhand. The server will go straight in for two steps, then cut back in order to cover the exposed area.

One finger tells the server the net man will poach. The server will run forward, as if the net man were crossing, and then return to normal approach.

Two fingers tells the server to place the ball as close to the middle of the court as possible. This tactic is used to minimize the angle of the opponent's return.

Signals worked out by one successful team are shown on page 70. Both players reviewed them constantly, for one very good reason: they didn't want to make mistakes. Nothing can make a team feel sillier—or make it look more foolish—than a tricky maneuver that backfires.

Figure 22.

Signaling to his partner, the net man turns his back to opponents and holds his hand on racket close to belt where sign cannot be stolen. One-finger sign given here tells the partner to fake a poach. The net man will move early on play, to tempt the receiver into hitting hurried shot down the line. His partner will fake to right and then go in.

THE TRICKY ART OF POACHING

The real object of all shots in doubles is to force the opponents to volley from beneath the level of the net. Both sides, therefore, must direct their strategy toward getting favorable put-away shots. Sometimes the conventional ways fail and a team must find new paths to the right shot.

The best and most direct is by poaching. Literally, one man infringes upon another's territory. This can either happen naturally in the course of play or it can be planned. If it is obvious that the net man can get the better-angled shot even though, by rights, the return belongs to his partner, he should take it. Partners who have played together for a long time know instinctively when each will poach on the other, but it is a good idea to signal a poach whenever possible. It is a better idea, of course, to follow the ball carefully at all times. If the poaching partner misses the ball, the other will be in position to cover for him.

A variation of the poach (and faked poach) is the drift.

Figure 23.

A. Ready to drift, the net man is in conventional position as ball is served.

A

B

B. After the ball passes him he begins to move along net. C. He continues to partner's court where he has excellent position for a

down-angled cross-court return. The server meanwhile crosses over to cover court vacated by partner.

C

Anticipating a cross-court return, the net man drifts, slowly at first, and then quickly, along the net toward the center of the court where he can drive a cross-court return for a winner.

Poaches and drifts can be used to fine effect as long as they are not overdone. Used in excess, however, they can make for poor doubles, drawing the players out of position too often and giving away their tactics. Moreover, they can run the legs off a team, since they require an uncommon amount of stopping and going. Poaching can also become trying if one partner hogs all the shots. Without a solid understanding between partners, no doubles team can win.

AUSTRALIAN FORMATION

If the receiver is making difficult cross-court returns, it is sometimes advantageous to use what is called the Australian formation. As seen in Figure 24, the net man is on the same side as the server, forcing the return to be made down the line. Best results usually come when the server places the ball on the receiver's backhand and closes in to volleying position at net.

Figure 24.

The Australian formation, shown in the two drawings on the opposite page, is a way around the difficulty caused by the serve to the backhand court. This formation works beautifully in protecting the weak backhand of the server. The server stands close to the center of court, taking the shortest route possible to probable volleying position. Variation of this formation permits the net man to drift across after the serve for interception of return with the server following the conventional approach to net.

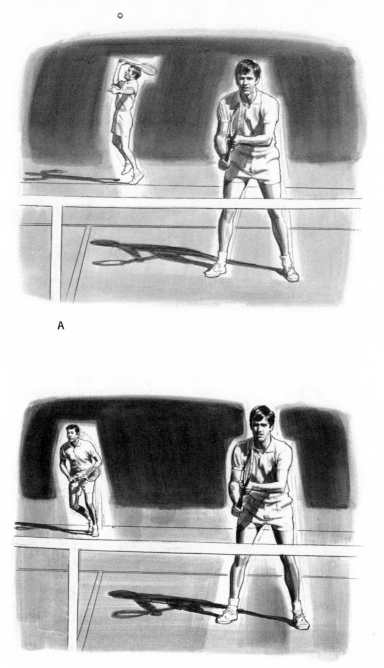

A

B

IMPORTANT POINTS TO REMEMBER IN DOUBLES

Pick a compatible partner, then concentrate on:

(1) Getting your first serve in deep in court.

(2) Returning every serve.

(3) Taking the net—the winning position—at every opportunity.

(4) Keeping the ball low with ground strokes and volleys, making your opponents hit up.

(5) Teaming together—individuality must give away to a coordinated team effort.

(6) Learning to anticipate your partner's and your opponents' moves.

(7) Hitting low down the middle when in doubt.

(8) Avoiding angled shots except for winners.

(9) Using the defensive lob when in deep trouble.

(10) Selecting the proper shot, placing it strategically, positioning yourself to deal with any return and developing an instinct that guides you to deal with the variety of circumstances you will face.

3
Mixed Doubles

MIXED DOUBLES, if played intelligently and accepted as a pleasant social interlude, can be great fun. It is an ideal way for husband and wife to team up and do something together during the summer months. Nancy and I have had a great deal of pleasure playing mixed doubles, so in this chapter I shall tell you some of the useful things I have learned.

Like marriage, mixed doubles is a give-and-take proposition. The smart team, as in the smart marriage, lets the man appear to be the boss. To be sure, the lady must carry her fair share of the burden—and even more on those not infrequent occasions when she is actually a better player than her partner. But one of the delightful facets of mixed doubles is that it can be played to the hilt without destroying the fundamental relationship between male and female. He can exercise his masculinity to the fullest. She can be athletic and still feminine.

The basic precepts of mixed doubles that I shall discuss here are just as applicable at Wimbledon as they are in a friendly match on the neighborhood court. First of all, the team should operate as a unit, remaining side by side in the backcourt or at net whenever possible, for it is only thus that you will both be at your best. When one or the other member of the team tries to dominate the court in doubles, it not only detracts from the fun but also creates confusion—and the team is that much less effective.

THE GOLDEN RULES

For Men

(1) Always ask your partner, "Would you like to serve first?" The courtesy is more important than the reply.

(2) If it is your team's turn to receive, stand firmly in the left court and ask her, "Which court do you prefer to play?"

(3) When your partner wrongly calls an opponent's shot out, don't correct her. Your opponents won't remember the favor, and she won't forgive you.

(4) Don't try to win all your points from the lady across the net. It's more rewarding to show up the other man.

(5) When the ball goes over the fence, fetch it on the trot. Women don't like men who are lazy.

(6) Never serve your hardest to the opposing lady unless she is patently a better player than you are. Use a spin serve; it looks soft but it is just as effective and nasty.

(7) If a crucial point is needed and the opposing lady is inept, take advantage of her glaring weakness but then protest you meant to hit it elsewhere.

(8) If your side wins, the drinks are on you.

(9) Always play your best; women are allergic to losing.

For Women

(1) Let your partner serve first. It will make him feel that victory depends on him.

(2) Play the right court when receiving (for the same reasons as above).

(3) Don't apologize when you miss. You didn't mean to make the error.

(4) Wear the most becoming outfit you can find in your wardrobe, but don't try to be too spectacular-looking. The too-intriguing costume can be as disconcerting to your partner as to your opponent. The undeviating color for tennis is white.

(5) Don't make your partner fetch all the loose balls around the court. He may abhor the helpless type.

(6) Compliment your partner generously but uneffusively when he makes a good shot. His ego is the key to his performance.

(7) Don't chat with the other players or the bystanders.

(8) Play the net uncomplainingly if your partner asks you to. He may have a reason.

(9) Always play your best; men prefer to win.

Doubles is a game where the attacking team always has the advantage. A team should constantly strive to attain and hold the net position, for it is there that a vast majority of the points are won. The advice that follows is predicated on the cardinal rules of doubles: work together, keep the pressure on your opponents and strive to reach the net where you will win your points.

THE IMPORTANCE OF A GOOD FIRST SERVE

It is an axiom of doubles—mixed or otherwise—that the server must win his serve or invite defeat. Figure 25 shows

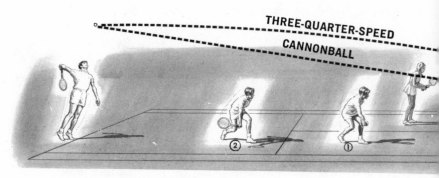

Figure 25. Three-Quarter-Speed Cannonball

how you can use the serve to gain an initial advantage in court tactics. You serve from a position midway between the center of the baseline and the doubles sideline, thus leaving yourself the shortest route to your proper position at net. Your partner, a good volleyer, stands halfway between the net and service line and about 10 feet in from the far sideline. For those who volley poorly it is advisable to play much closer to the net; the less agile should play much closer to the sideline to protect the alley. But even a poor volleyer should play the net when the partner is serving, for this formation offers a psychological salient that more than offsets any shortcomings on the part of the net player.

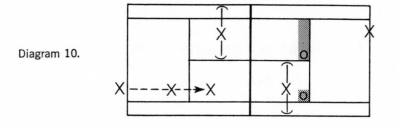

Diagram 10.

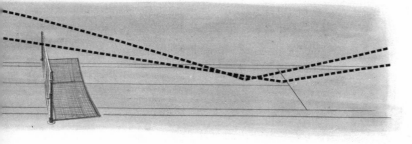

It is most important to get your first serve in, and you will find that a three-quarter-speed serve not only gives you greater control but also allows you more time to reach the net (position 1)—three priceless steps farther than you would get from a hard, flat cannonball that can be returned to you while you are still in no-man's-land between the baseline and service line (position 2). To protect your partner at net, always serve deep (into the shaded areas of Diagram 10) and preferably to the receiver's backhand (circles on diagram), where the odds favor a weaker return. These fundamentals apply equally to the right and left courts.

THE DEFENSIVE LOB WHEN IN TROUBLE

If your opponents are serving well—or you are serving weakly—you will quickly find yourself on the defensive in the backcourt. It is here that you will find the lob, particularly the defensive lob, most useful in extricating yourself from trouble. The server has played a shot deep and wide to your backhand, leaving you and your partner extremely vulnerable. Your opponents are waiting eagerly at net in good position to end the point. A very high defensive lob (see Diagram 11) is your proper shot, and it should be played as deep as possible. This will give you and your partner time to regain your best defensive formation before the return comes back.

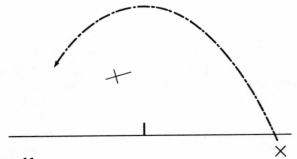

Diagram 11.

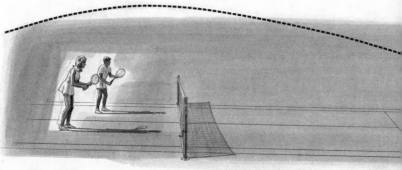

Figure 26.

THE OFFENSIVE LOB TO REGAIN THE NET

In Figure 26, your opponents have control of the net and are crowding it closely in hopes of ending the rally with a sharp volley off one of your returns. Although both you and your partner are in the backcourt, you are in good position and hence able to assume the attack whenever a useful opportunity presents itself. This is an excellent strategic moment for the offensive lob that will drive your opponents back and permit you and your partner to grab the net position. The offensive lob, as distinguished from the defensive, is played low—low but very deep. Sure disaster lies in running to the net after a low lob that is too

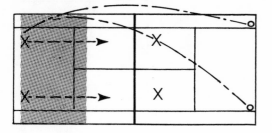

Diagram 12.

short. The opponents will just slam it at your feet while you are in no-man's-land (shaded area in Diagram 12), and there is nothing you can do about that.

Whenever possible, it is best to place the offensive lob on the backhand side of either of your opponents. Few tennis players have the ability to hit a forceful overhead from the backhand. (I often purposely lob low to the backhand of a player at net, forcing him back slightly into his own vulnerable no-man's-land.) Since you can then almost surely bank on a weak return, you and your partner then follow the shot to net knowing you will most likely catch your opponents in a bad position and will have a good chance to win the point.

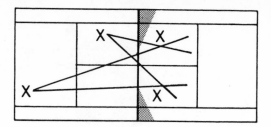

Diagram 13.

WHEN IN DOUBT—PLAY THE MIDDLE

Although the net is the position from which you will win the most points, it is by no means impregnable. Your net position is proper, and a passing shot to the outside, where the net is 6 inches higher, would be extremely risky (see shaded areas in Diagram 13). Eschewing the lob, your opponents have chosen to play the safe percentage shot down the middle, keeping it low. There is no need to hit this shot hard; use only as much speed as you can control. Since the shot has been played low, it will be impossible for you to volley it offensively for a winner, so all you can hope to do is return it deep enough to keep your opponents back and not lose the net for your side. Since you can cover the middle with your forehand, the down-the-middle shot is definitely your responsibility; but it would have been your partner's job if your positions had been reversed and she were in the left-hand court.

PROTECTING A WEAK BACKHAND

I am a firm believer in the axiom: if losing, change tactics. In Diagram 14, where your partner is serving from the left-hand court, you move over to the same side to protect her backhand. Your opponent in the left-hand court is making beautiful cross-court returns of your partner's serve, and she is having trouble with the low backhand volleys and

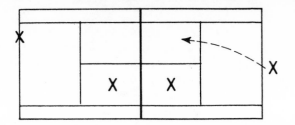

Diagram 14.

half volleys she had to make in following her serve to net. She now will run up to the net position on her stronger, forehand side. (See illustrations on page 75.)

Figure 27.

THE POACHER CAN BE BOTH GOOD AND BAD

The poach is a vital play in doubles, but not unless done with the full cooperation and consent of your partner. When you're going to poach, alert your partner by placing your racket behind your back or saying something like, "You're playing like a dream, dear." This is her (his) cue to cover you from behind in case the maneuver backfires.

The worst menace on the court is the "bully" poacher who dashes back and forth at net, leaving his partner bewildered. But there is a cure for him: Hit it right at his middle (see solid line in Diagram 15), down the alley he has just vacated, or over his head (dotted line). He'll get the message, and there will be more fun for all.

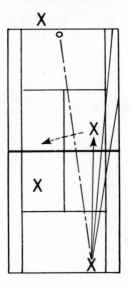

Diagram 15.

Glossary of Tennis Terms

ACE. A serve the receiver is unable to get his racket on—the equivalent of a strikeout pitch in baseball. The word is also used as a verb: The server aces his opponent.

AD. A common abbreviation of the word "advantage," used in keeping score after a game reaches deuce. If Laver wins the next point after deuce, for example, the score is given as "Advantage Laver" or, less formally, "Laver's ad."

AD-IN. A scorekeeping term that omits the server's name but indicates that the score is his ad. If Laver, while serving, wins the next point after deuce, the score is "Advantage Laver" or "ad-in." Add-out is the opposite of ad-in.

ALLEY. The area, 4.5 feet wide, added to each side of a singles court to make it a doubles court.

AMERICAN TWIST. A spin serve delivered with a snap of the wrist that causes the ball, after landing in the service court, to kick off sharply to the receiver's left when delivered by a right-handed server.

ANGLE VOLLEY. A stroke hit before the ball touches the ground and angled past an opponent.

APPROACH SHOT. A running-in shot behind which a player advances to the net. He hits it deep to give him time to get there.

BACKCOURT. The area, 18 feet deep, between the service line and the baseline.

BACKSPIN. A rotary motion applied by undercutting the ball so that it spins in the opposite direction of its flight path. Also called *underspin.*

BASELINE. The rear boundary at each end of the court.

CANNONBALL. A flat, powerful serve given maximum speed.

CHOP. A stroke in which the ball is given underspin or backspin. Also called *chip.*

CONTINENTAL GRIP. A compromise about halfway between the eastern forehand and eastern backhand grips, used by some players to eliminate the necessity of shifting their hand on the racket. It is also called the *service grip* because it's the grip most commonly used in serving.

CROSS-COURT SHOT. A ball hit diagonally to the opposite side of the court.

CROSS-OVER. A tactic employed by the serving team in doubles, in which the net man moves across the center in a poach and the server follows a diagonal path to the net to cover the court vacated by his partner. Also called *scissors.*

DEUCE. An even score after 3 or more points have been won by each player or team in a game. A score of 40–40 is deuce. A deuce set is an even score in games after ten or more are played.

DINK. A general term for any kind of spin shot plopped softly over the net.

DOUBLE FAULT. The failure of the server—which costs him the point—to put either his first or second service into play.

DOWN-THE-LINE-SHOT. One that is hit roughly parallel to the sideline.

DRIFT. A variation of the poach, in which the net man on the serving team in doubles edges toward the center of the court—first slowly, then more quickly—to a position where he can handle a cross-court return.

DRIVE. A shot hit with a full stroke, either forehand or backhand, after the bounce.

DROP SHOT. A soft stroke hit with backspin that lands just beyond the net.

DROP VOLLEY. A drop shot hit off a ball on the fly. Also called *stop volley*.

FAULT. The failure of the server to put his first serve in play.

FLAT SERVE. One that is given very little spin and consequently hard to control.

FOOT FAULT. A fault called on a server for stepping on or over the baseline before his racket touches the ball.

FORCING SHOT. Any shot with which one player assumes the initiative, forcing his opponent into an error or weak return or putting him in an awkward position.

FORECOURT. The area, 21 feet deep, between the net and the service court.

GAME. The unit of scoring between the point and the set. It takes 4 points to win a game, six games to win a set—unless either the game or the set reaches deuce, in which case play continues indefinitely until someone gets 2 points (or two games) ahead.

GROUND STROKE. Any shot hit after it has bounced, as opposed to a volley, which is hit on the fly.

HALF-VOLLEY. A misleading name for a pick-up shot, a ball hit immediately after it bounces—misleading because a volley, by definition, is a ball hit on the fly.

LET. Any stroke that for some reason is replayed without penalty. The most common type of let is a serve that ticks the net but lands in the proper court. Sometimes this is mistakenly referred to as a "net" serve; the accurate term is "let."

LOB. Any ball lofted high in the air, usually over the head of an opponent. Offensive lobs are meant to win points outright by surprising an opponent too close to the net. Defensive lobs, which are usually hit much higher, are intended to allow enough time to recover from a vulnerable position. (In England and Australia, the lob is called a "toss.")

LOVE. A scoring term synonymous with "zero" or "nothing."

MATCH. A competition between two players or teams that consists of a predetermined number of sets or games.

MATCH POINT. The last point to win a match.

NET BALL. Any shot after the serve that touches the net but remains in play.

NET GAME. A style of play that depends largely on overheads and volleys hit from a position near the net.

NETCORD. A shot hit into the tape at the top of the net which rolls over and falls on the opposite side, thereby deciding the point.

NO-MAN'S-LAND. The area between the baseline and the service line where lingering is ill advised.

OVERHEAD. A ball smashed from a high position off a lob.

PASSING SHOT. A ball that an opponent playing near the net is unable to get his racket on.

PLACEMENT. Any shot hit out of an opponent's reach.

POACH. The invasion by one member of a doubles team of his partner's normal territory.

"PUT AWAY." To hit a shot so well that no return can be made.

RALLY. A relatively long exchange of shots before a point is finally decided.

"READ." To anticipate accurately an opponent's moves, usually with the help of small clues. A player who is reading his adversary well enjoys a decided advantage.

RETRIEVER. A player who excels at running down and returning hard shots.

REVERSE BACKWARD. A shot hit backward over the net by a player facing the other direction.

SERVE, SERVICE. The act of putting the ball into play.

SERVICE COURT. The area in which the serve must land for

the ball to be in play. Each service court, left and right, is 21 feet deep and 13.5 feet wide. The service courts for doubles are the same as for singles.

SERVICE LINE. The back boundary of the service courts, 21 feet from the net.

SET. The unit of scoring between the game and the match. Six games win a set unless the games stand five-all, in which case play continues until someone gets two ahead.

SET POINT. The last point needed to win a set.

SIDE-BY-SIDE FORMATION. The normal alignment after the service in doubles, as contrasted to the outdated one-up-and-one-back system.

SIDE SERVICE LINE. The outside boundary of the service court. In singles, the side service line is also the sideline.

SIDELINES. The left and right boundaries of the playing surface.

SITTER. Any shot that hangs invitingly in the air, easy to return for a winner.

SLICE. A stroke to which heavy sidespin is imparted. It breaks to a right-handed player's left as he delivers it.

SMASH. An overhead stroke hit forcefully, intended to win the point outright.

SPIN. The rotating motion of the ball in any direction.

STOP VOLLEY. A drop shot hit on the fly; a drop volley.

"SWEET SPOT." The area in the center of the racket head—ideally, the section of the strings that strikes the ball. A stroke launched from the sweet spot carries maximum pace and is easier to control than one hit near the rim.

TANDEM FORMATION. Another name for the *Australian Formation* (see pp. 74–75).

THREE-BOUNCE RULE. A modification of the official rules that encourages longer rallies. It prohibits both players from advancing to the net until the ball has bounced three times.

TOPSPIN. A rotary motion, imparted to the ball by stroking up and over it, which accentuates the forward movement of the ball. Also called *overspin*.

TOSS. In America, the act of throwing the ball up before serving it. In England and Australia, a high-lofted shot —what Americans call a lob.

TWIST. A serve hit with a combination of topspin and sidespin, which gives the ball a kicking action off the ground.

VOLLEY. Any stroke hit on the fly, before it bounces.

WESTERN GRIP. An outmoded manner of holding the racket, awkward for returning low shots.